Straight From My Heart
by
5 February 2005 **Bill Holmes**

To Jerome Glover —

Thank you for your support! It is always an honor & a pleasure to share the mic with a gentleman like yourself! May you always be Blessed in your endeavors!

Best Wishes,

SFMH

Published by
Universal Expressions, LLC
First Edition
First Printing

Published by Universal Expressions, LLC
P.O. Box 7801
Philadelphia, PA 19101
www.universalexpressions.com

Copyright (c) 2002 by William L Holmes, Jr.

Editors: Uva Anckle and Tonya Marie Evans
Cover Art Design: Bernard Collins
Book Layout: Bernard Thorn/BMT Pictorials

Holmes, William L, Jr.
Pseudonym: Bill Holmes
Straight From My Heart
ISBN Trade: 0-9716757-0-8

Table of Contents

let's keep it together …

maybe we can …

to all good things ...

Dedication

This book is dedicated to the memory of my grandparents, Samuel and Mazie Jones. You were the flames that gave our family life, strength, guidance, and inspiration to strive towards excellence. May the Lord bless and watch over your eternal souls. I miss you and I love you.

Acknowledgments

First and foremost, I must give thanks to God for being the light of my life! Thank You for being my Savior and for the wonderful blessings You have bestowed upon me!

To my parents, William L. Holmes Sr. and Sandra L. Baytops, thank you for being the foundation of my strength and inspiration! I could not have asked for two better individuals to raise me to become the man I am today!

To Tanya Dinkins, thank you for being my best friend! There are no words to describe how special you are to me!

To Uva Anckle, thank you for showing me the true value of friendship! You are a ray of sunshine that has touched my life! ¡Abrazos!

To Gene and Kymm Roberson, thank you for showing me the true power of love and its infinite possibilities! Congratulations on the birth of your son, Miles, who is an extension of your beautiful spirits!

To Angela Kinamore, thank you for your enthusiastic encouragement! You've shown me poetry is greater than any human being on this planet, but friendship is a divine blessing!

To Deon Browning, thank you for the "Old School" knowledge "Young William" needs to hear every now and then! You are a blessed brotha and I wish you nothing but peace and prosperity!

To Bernard Collins, thank you for the PHAT book cover! Your genius, kindness, and vision are unparalleled and there is no one quite like you, Nard!

To Tonya Marie Evans, thank you for letting the world witness your SHINE! Your family's unselfish commitment to bring this art to a new level is opening many doors, and I am grateful for your accomplishments!

To Khaliq Johnson, thank you for the enlightening conversations we've shared on the road! Your energy, creativity, and perseverance breathe life into my words!

To Bernard Thorn, thank you for the cover and text layout! Your patience and determination brought this project to life and I thank you!

To Lamont Steptoe, thank you for the lessons I've learned under your tutelage! You've taught me how to appreciate the beauty and the language of poetry!

To Lamont "NAPALM" Dixon, thank you for being a talented poet, a mentor, and a gentleman! Your accomplishments inspire me to be the best positive role model for our young Black children! KABOOM!

To Marcus Major, thank you for paving the way for aspiring writers like myself! Your kind words gave me faith to achieve my dreams!

To Kimmika Williams, thank you for suggesting this idea to me on June 26, 1999! It is always an honor and a privilege to share the same stage with you, Diva!

To Tantra, thank you for giving me the courage to write! You are living proof a lotus does indeed blossom into a lovely flower! One Love!

To Stephanie Lee, thank you for the laughs we've shared! Keep striving for the moon, Chef Boyarlee, because we'll soon be among the stars! Woo, woo, woo!

To Rochelle Reynolds, thank you for your assistance, advice, and friendship! You have a beautiful gift the world needs to hear and I wish you all the best in your endeavors, my Sister in Christ!

To Carla Thompson-Pinion, thank you for your generosity and sweetness! You are an angel that showers the world with your love! Woo, woo, woo!

To Osay Karume, thank you for being the big brother I always needed! Get ready to pack you bags 'cause our next getaway is going to be IG'NANT! OH, YOU DON'T KNOW!

To Crystal Alston, thank you for being my buddy and for the brotha/sista (or sista/brotha) conversations we've shared! You are a blessed and beautiful lady, Kid, who will ALWAYS have a place in my heart!

To Donna Bennett and Sandra Walls, thank you for being my adoptive mothers! Your heartwarming e-mails and anecdotes know how to bring a smile to my face when I'm feeling blue!

To the RECAP Book club, thank you for the mad love! Our gatherings are too comical and they are definitely not for the weak at heart!

To Sophia Delva and Richelle Woodard, thank you for being my sisters over the years! I can never forget you ladies the way you forget my birthday every year! GOTCHA!

I would like to give special thanks to the following poets, artists, singers, and writers for their dedication, passion, and commitment: Jill Scott, Saul Williams, Jessica Care Moore, Nikki Giovanni, Taalam Acey, Faraji Saalim, Lamar Hill, Lois Moses, Maurice Henderson, Angela Moore, Valerie Banks, Reggie Gibson, Kwame Alexander, Stephanie Renee and the CCP Ink Family, Tiffany Bacon, J. Michael Harrison, Demetrius tha Poet, LaDayne, Tamara Davis, Chuma Whahid Rasul, Precious Gift, Samori, Tranzit Thawt, the Unknown Poet and Queen, Nikki Taylor, Lady Danco, Oree, Shafiyq, Sam I Am, Charles Armstrong, Rom Wills, Althea Hughes, DuEwa Frazier, Eric Frazier, Margie Shaheed, Sandra Turner Barnes, D. Ryva Parker, Ron Carter, Eric Webb, In The Company of Poets, the Mad Poets Society, the Twin Poets, the Last Poets, and Amiri and Amini Baraka.

To everyone who has supported me in all of my poetic endeavors, thank you so much! There are too many individuals for me to name, but I have ONE LOVE FOR EVERYBODY! Please keep me in your thoughts and prayers because you are in mine! Straight from my heart, Bill!

Introduction

Straight From My Heart is a collection of poetry and essays that represent the reflections, observations, emotions, and experiences of one human being in this journey of life and its infinite possibilities. This project has been three and a half years in the making and has been worth every ounce of my creativity, determination, and perseverance to capture a piece of my soul in the spoken and the written word.

Writing has been my true love and there is no greater sensation that brings me fulfillment, prosperity, and tranquility than putting my thoughts to paper. I could not have ever imagined that my words would bring many opportunities and blessings that have come into my life: having the ability to touch another person's life in a positive way; meeting many talented poets and writers whose words give me inspiration to write and to read; being able to discover self-esteem and to appreciate the beauty and the power of love. A friend of mine once wrote "it is truly an honor to share my writing with you and I thank God for His blessings and unconditional love...all praise to the Most High," and I could not have agreed more with her statement.

desperate times, desperate situations ...

Unbelievable

41 SHOTS
discharged from the smoking barrels
of 4 undercover cops,
19 BULLETS tearing into 1 man's flesh,
piercing through his limbs and his chest,
another innocent victim
SLAUGHTERED
in the prime of his life
by the fascist and the racist cowards
who hide their childhood insecurities
behind copper badges of shame
in this senseless game
of police brutality coming soon
to your neighborhood
regardless of "whether you've been bad or good,"
because you are BORN BLACK
and you are a BORN SUSPECT
presumed GUILTY of a crime
YOU DIDN'T COMMIT,
"AmeriKKKa's worst nightmare,"
striving to build a better life
for yourself and your loved ones
as the police greet you
at the front door of your home
to welcome you with loaded firearms
and a black body bag
at 5 o'clock in the morning ...

BOOM,
BOOM, BOOM,
BOOM, BOOM, BOOM, BOOM, BOOM, BOOM, BOOM,
BOOM, BOOM, BOOM, BOOM, BOOM, BOOM, BOOM,
BOOM, BOOM, BOOM, BOOM, BOOM, BOOM, BOOM,
BOOM, BOOM, BOOM, BOOM, BOOM, BOOM, BOOM,
BOOM, BOOM, BOOM, BOOM, BOOM, BOOM, BOOM,
BOOM, BOOM,
BOOM!

another innocent victim
SLAUGHTERED
in the prime of his life
by the fascists and the racist cowards
who hide their childhood insecurities
behind copper badges of shame
in this senseless game
of police brutality
where there is no justice
for JUST US
as history repeats itself
in the new millennium.

Trust Me

"Don't be afraid son,"
my dad told me before he
fondled my penis.

C2D

Tomorrow is just
another day not promised
to young Black children.

Shattered Dreams

Sunlit glass lying
on asphalt streets covered by
a harmless child's blood.

Sunglasses

Ray Ban shades disguise
the black eye on her brown face,
but can't hide the pain.

The Cooking Pot

The flame
is extinguished
but the kettle still brews,
boils, and bubbles just waiting to
explode.

Helping Hands

Someone
is crying for
help tonight but no one
listens if it benefits their
wallets.

Drowning

One, two,
three, four, five, six
shots of tequila are
no laughing matter when you lose
control.

Open Fire

Bullets
shot into the
crowd have no regard to
race, creed, class, or the color of
your skin!

Strange Days

Is it just me,
or is it just one of those days
I should have stayed in bed?
Or maybe, I'm still asleep
and this is a vivid nightmare
I can't wake up from,
as crime and corruption continue to rise
while peace and innocence
are swirling down
that liquid whirlpool inside my toilet
along with society's morals and ethics?
Sometimes I have to ask myself
"What's Goin' On?" like Marvin Gaye,
because can someone tell me
how mothers can abandon their newborn infants
in trash containers like yesterday's newspaper
and fathers can rape their children
downstairs in their basements
and walk away from the scene of the crime
with a slap on the wrist?
Can you justify to me
how cocaine is funneled into Amish communities
and the FBI decides to sit back on its ambitions
and instead raid urban neighborhoods
while everybody in Lancaster, PA
is happy and high with Weird Al
"living in an Amish paradise?"
Can someone please explain to me
how lunatics and white supremacists
enlist in the armed forces
to learn how to devise strategies,
to operate nuclear weapons,

to overthrow the government,
and to annihilate all people of color?

Maybe I should go to the bookstore
and read a good book to find
the answers I'm looking for,
but every book I find on the shelf
is a 600 page, college thesis
written by a pseudo intellectual,
African American author
who wasn't "born in the ghetto,"
who hasn't "been to the ghetto,"
who doesn't "understand the ghetto,"
but proposes solutions to the ghetto
while reaping the profits
of his bestseller's royalties
and educating the masses
at Ivy League institutions!

Maybe I should just chill out
and go to the movies or watch some TV,
but the more things change,
the more things remain the same,
because brothas are STILL being portrayed
as slaves, sidekicks, sambos,
drug dealers, hoodlums, and convicts,
while sistas have progressed
from mammies and maids
to prostitutes and strippers,
as Black actors are being forced
to compromise their integrity
by fulfilling the childhood fantasies
of Hollywood executives
from the glory days

of Saturday afternoon
Tarzan movie matinees
and masturbating in their bedrooms
while looking through
National Geographic magazines
to land good parts in Tinseltown,
and it broke my heart
watching Esther Rolle,
God rest her eternal soul,
selling psychic hotline commercials
on Black Entertainment Television!

"DAMN! DAMN! DAMN!"

Maybe I should heed Jill Scott's advice
and "take a long walk" outside
to clear my head and to gather my thoughts,
but I go inside the local grocery store
and I see merchants selling
malt liquor and tobacco cigarettes
to underage adolescents.
I look across the street
and I see new jack hustlers selling
the latest bootleg DVDs and CDs
in front of police stations.
Six blocks down the street
the United States Government
is distributing drugs and firearms
to our children at the playground,
but a Black man is beaten down
and arrested in broad daylight
for jaywalking across the street?

Maybe I need to go to church
and get down on my knees
and say a prayer,
but guess who I see
sitting in the pulpit...
The Devil himself,
grinning from ear to ear
and watching his handiwork
unfold before his bloodshot eyes.
The Ten Commandments are thrown out
of the stained glass window
and have been replaced by the Seven Deadly Sins;
deacons are fondling their neighbors' wives,
preachers are extorting a few dollars
from the collection plate,
and the entire congregation has been
corrupted by envy, fornication,
gossip, and hearsay.
We're no longer marching to Zion,
but are headed down a highway
straight into Hell
with rest stops
in Sodom and Gommorah!

Is it just me,
or is it just one of
those days of our lives
when the "sand is running
through the hourglass"
and the final countdown
to Judgment Day has begun?
Or maybe, it's not too late
to smell the coffee and wake up
because time is on our side
and we still have one chance
to get it together
once...and for all?
Can somebody please
let me know?

looking on the bright side ...

Survivor

The roar of the thunder
and the fury of the raindrops
splattering against my window
awaken me from my sleep
as sweat emerges from my pores,
cascading down every inch of my skin
like branches of a turbulent river
and my body trembles,
and my heart beats rapidly
as I run the race of my life
on this restless night.

Temptations are strong tonight,
oh yes, they are DAMN STRONG,
to have that one drink,
to smoke that one joint,
to take that one hit,
and to alleviate/eradicate/sedate
the burden of carrying
the weight of a world
that despises me
from my tired shoulders.

All I need is one high,
just one more high
to escape from the reality
of these inner city blues
that has a stranglehold
upon my life and to watch
all of my anger and my anxieties,
all of my fears and my frustrations
disappear... right before my eyes...

but the teardrops
falling down my face
won't allow me to succumb
to weakness
and to fall
from grace.

Every battle
to remain pure and clean
in mind, body, and spirit
is a daily struggle I wrestle with
and becomes more difficult
in this everlasting war
that rages inside my soul
as the demons of my past
continue to torment me
and are watching me,
and are waiting for me
to make that one mistake,
to slip into my old habits,
and to slide down
that spiral staircase
towards my

but my enemies
have underestimated my strength
because they did not MAKE ME,
therefore they can not BREAK ME!

And I hear the voices
of the Doubting Thomases
and the skeptics inside my head
"it is so easy to talk the talk, my brotha,
can you walk the walk?"
because some do not believe in me,
some have abandoned me,
some do not care about me,
but I believe in myself,
my loved ones are there for me,
and God still loves me
and by no means is He
FINISHED WITH ME
and every step I take
with faith and courage by my side,
I will continue to strive
until the day I die...
TO SURVIVE...
      TO SURVIVE...
            TO SURVIVE!!!

Striving

The wind against my
face does not prevent me from
finishing the race.

Hope

A crack of sunlight
falling through the dark skies is
my motivation.

Little Black Boys

Little Black boys
are being taught by their schoolteachers
they don't possess the mental capacity
to become doctors, lawyers, and engineers,
and our young prodigies are being denied
their opportunity to shine
and find themselves without a prayer
since that's been removed from the classroom
and are caught up in the aftermath
of the new era of Reaganomics and gangsta rap
where only the strong survive
by committing urban genocide:
selling drugs in their communities
"to get that dolla, dolla bill, y'all,"
or taking another human being's life
with a gun because someone approached them
on the streets and just said
"Hello!"

Little Black boys
are being abandoned
by triflin' ass, mack daddy,
2 minute brothas who can't
tell the difference between
a wedding ring and a condom
as deadbeat dads are turning their backs
on their sons when they need them the most
because these jackasses don't know
the first thing about being
neither a father nor a man,
and decide to live their lives
as 20 to 50 year old adolescents

while little Black boys are left
to fend for themselves
in a global cauldron of sin and corruption,
fueled by the fiery flames
of racism, misery, and poverty
with some adversity and animosity thrown in
because of the color of their skin,
sexual preference, and choice of religion
that's slowly boiling towards Armageddon.

Little Black boys
are being told that
the only chance they have to attain
their piece of the American dream
is to become a basketball player
or a hardcore rapper
and are being spoon fed
hoop dreams to "be like Mike"
along with derogatory hip hop rhymes
that insult their mothers and sisters
by calling them "bitches" and "hoes"
as their gullible minds
are being deceived by the powers that be
because they don't realize no athlete
with a multimillion dollar sneaker contract
can move a muscle or make a decision
without Corporate America's permission,
and you can be nominated for a Grammy
by acting like a park ape
"stylin' and profilin'"
in a 3 piece gorilla suit
with a $1 million dollar smile
full of gold teeth
but at the end of the show

you'll be shut out in the cold,
standing up on stage with no awards
crying about being all dressed up
with no place to go.

Little Black boys
NEED to be taught and told
they are the sons of Malcolm and Betty,
they are the recipients of Martin's dream,
and they were NOT marked for
exploitation or extermination
but were marked for EXCELLENCE
in the eyes of the Lord
before they were born
because "hope is alive" and breathing
within their spirits and can only be
manifested through love, pride,
respect, and encouragement
and it is not our duty
but it is our responsibility as adults
to teach them these values
because little Black boys
are the Nubian torchbearers
that will carry that flame
into this new millennium
to lead our people
to the Promised Land!

Caribbean Blues

My eyes yearn to watch
the red sun set over the
enchanting, blue sea.

The Dream

I was standing alone on the deck of a cruise ship overlooking the sun set upon Montego Bay. My God! What an awesome sight it was! I've seen sunsets at many beaches across the United States, but this was truly a SUNSET! The sun looked like a gigantic red ball of fire descending upon the sea. I could feel the diminishing heat of its invisible rays on my skin. The water was so clear and had the prettiest shade of blue I've ever seen. The air smelled so fresh I felt rejuvenated as I inhaled the aroma of the salt water into my lungs. The sounds of the chirping seagulls flying above in the sky pacified my soul. This was one of life's precious moments that could not be captured in a photograph or on videotape because film would not do it any justice.

I began to recall my favorite moment from Octavia Butler's Wild Seed. It was the sensation the heroine, Anyanwu, experienced when she transformed herself into a dolphin and swam in the Atlantic Ocean during her journey from Africa to the American colonies aboard the slave vessel. Suddenly, I felt a need to take off my clothes. And I did so without shame. I climbed on top of the ship's rail and, naked as a newborn child, I stood on its warm metal ledge. I closed my eyes, took a deep breath, and dove headfirst into the Caribbean Sea.

My entire body began to transform into the shape of a dolphin. I swam away from the ship and began to explore the wonderful and mysterious environment with my heightened senses. I heard the sounds of little Jamaican children playing on the beach miles away on the shore. The further I drifted from the sunlight, I felt the water's temperature fluctuate and my body adapted to the change. I saw seashells, coral reefs and other species of fish moving in different directions around me.

I FELT ALIVE for the first time in my life! I could not explain this sensation because it was difficult to define my feelings with words. Adrenaline rushed through every nerve and every muscle as I swam with reckless abandon. My dolphin-like body jumped into the sky and fell back into the water, singing songs I never heard before. I kept repeating this feat in a desperate attempt to reach for the clouds. With each jump, it seemed as if I was getting closer to achieving my goal until I heard the sound of the telephone ringing.

I woke up from my sleep entangled in the baby blue covers of my bed. I picked up the telephone only to hear a recording of my voice telling me to get out of bed and go to work. I looked at the alarm clock sitting on my nightstand. It displayed "6:30 A.M." in luminous, green digits.

"Damn! It was just a dream," I muttered as I looked at my body-human and familiar and clothed in cranberry red pajamas. But it was more than a dream because I felt I had been there. I climbed out of bed and looked through my bedroom window. The orange sun was ascending above the white clouds and into the light blue sky. I closed my eyes and said a prayer thanking God for allowing me to see another day.

Beauty

Like a lotus
she grows and blossoms
into a lovely flower
in spite of the mud
that surrounds her life
while she matures
into full bloom.

As a child,
she was the unfortunate victim
of vicious attacks and verbal assaults
upon her innocent soul
because of the color of her skin
and the texture of her hair.
She was the butt of all the jokes
at the playgrounds and the schoolyards
by the other children growing up
in her neighborhood in North Philly.
She was the recipient
of harsh beatings and severe tongue lashings
by her parents because she was told
she was the ugliest child
in her family.

As an adult,
our society attempts
to place many hats
upon her pretty head
she wishes neither to wear
nor to acknowledge.
She is the resentment
of her confused sistas

who can't distinguish
between reality and fantasy
by impersonating
their Caucasian counterparts.
She is the object of disgust
to the small minded brothas
who will not give her
the time of day,
but become green with envy
and criticize her for dating
outside of her race.
She is the "Foxy Brown,"
"Black Coffee,"
"Hot Chocolate" sexual fantasy
to the perverted knuckleheads
who will give her the world
and will love her all day, all night
OUT OF SIGHT
from their family and friends.

If you close your eyes,
open your mind
and look straight into her heart,
you will see she's a human being
like you and I,
looking for some love and respect
in a complex, color stricken world
where one is judged first
upon their physical appearance
and not what lies within.
But you see, she is more
than a human being;
She is BEAUTY,
a natural phenomenon
and wonder of this great universe!
She is the serene Moon
overlooking the Earth
from the stars above,
a spectacular sight
that leaves you spellbound!
She is the purple haze
that blankets the morning sky
of a new day that rejuvenates
the spirit of life!
She is the eternal waterfall
that cascades down
the magical mountains
of the Brazilian rainforest,
the personification
of Mother Nature's
graceful harmony!

Every place I travel to
and everywhere I look,
I see BEAUTY
in her many
marvelous incarnations
that brings me to my knees
to give thanks and praise
to the Almighty:
I see BEAUTY
in the dreams of little Black girls
playing hopscotch and double dutch
at the after school programs
where their imaginations
know no boundaries!
I see BEAUTY
in the determination
of single Black mothers
who rise every morning
and maintain their mental stability
after working 60 hours and 2 jobs
to build promising futures
for their children!
I see BEAUTY
in the strength
of former prom queens
turned recovering crack addicts
who exorcise their demons
to rebuild their shattered lives
by rising from DISGRACE
to AMAZING GRACE!
I see BEAUTY
in the achievement
of 63 year old grandmothers
who fulfill their lifetime goal

of obtaining college degrees
by overcoming obstacles
such as racism, family commitments
and poverty!
I see BEAUTY
in all of my sistas
for everything they are
and for everything they do
because they are and will always be
BEAUTY
and from this Black man's heart,
I salute you!

5 February 2001

Dear God,

Thank You for allowing me to see another day. I would like to give You thanks and praise for the wonderful blessings You have bestowed upon me. It feels fantastic to be alive and to cherish the beautiful aspects life offers: sunrises and sunsets; family and friends; rain and snow; and most importantly, You, O Precious Lord. I'll be fortunate to have the morning chill touch my cheeks when I go to work today even though I dislike both cold weather and Mondays.

I would like to say a prayer, God, for myself because lately I've been caught up in the ugliness and negativity of doubt, anger, loneliness, and narcissism. My time on this planet is too short and too precious to waste by being burdened with these bitter feelings taking their toll on my well being. I have so much to live for because I am alive and breathing and that is a major accomplishment.

I am committed to learn to love and to appreciate myself more each and every day because I am worthy and deserving of Your unconditional love. Your unconditional love has been the foundation of my strength and my inspiration for the 31 years of my existence. Your unconditional love has always forgiven me when my words, thoughts, and actions disrespected You, my family, my friends, and myself. Your unconditional love has comforted me during my darkest moments when I felt alone, depressed, hurt, rejected, or miserable because of the actions of individuals who, intentionally or unintentionally, abused my friendship, generosity or affection.

Your unconditional love has shown me there is no greater power in this universe than You, God, and without You, I AM NOTHING!

Thank You, God, for being my Savior. In Jesus' precious name I pray. Amen.

Love,

Bill Holmes

let's keep it together …

Mama's Smile

The first sight my eyes had seen,
the inspiration of my hopes and dreams.

A picture no words can describe,
beautiful as a black butterfly.

An image that evokes harmony,
majestic like the African Safari.

A vision descended from Heaven above,
the reflection of God's unconditional love.

A grin, serene like the River Nile,
that warms my heart, my Mama's smile.

Dad

In a time and place
where heroes were needed, I
thank God you were mine.

Heartbeat

I know you can hear
the sound of my heart beating
when I think of you
as I look up
at the royal blue sky
where the angels
and all of God's children roam,
and I know you're out there
somewhere
watching down upon me
from the gates of Heaven
with your smiling eyes.

And I absolutely feel no shame
when I'm no longer able
to hold back
the tears in my eyes
every time I look
at your photograph
and see your beautiful face,
and my mind travels back
to my childhood days
as fond memories
flash before my eyes
of all the precious moments
we spent together as a family
celebrating birthdays and holidays,
or me being the recipient
of scoldings and whippings
whenever I stepped out of line.

And deep down inside
I wish I could have
one last chance
to turn back
the hands of time
so I can hear your sweet voice
in my ears calling my name,
so I can taste your homemade
German chocolate cake
and buttermilk pancakes in my mouth,
so I can hug you in my arms
and to tell you how much
I love you and I miss you
because I didn't
have the chance
to say goodbye.
And on the day you died,
a part of me died,
and my life
has never been the same.

And I know you can feel
the pride inside of me
because your blood
flows through my veins
and your legacy lives
through my accomplishments
and although my mother
will always be my inspiration,
your spirit gave me LIFE
because you were the one
who told me that I was
"YOUNG, GIFTED, AND BLACK"
and NOBODY can take that
away from me!

You were the one
who taught me
to always believe
in my dreams
because if I believe,
then I can achieve
anything I desire
and straight from my heart,
I THANK YOU!

Perfect Strangers

A husband and wife
no longer see eye to eye,
and can't explain why?

Dreaming

I want to feel
the power of
your loving arms
wrapped around my body
in my moments of weakness
when I need the warmth
of your comforting presence
to bring me security.

I want to look
into your deep, smoky eyes
and to exchange my thoughts
with your fascinating mind
because my spirit yearns
to dance in the spotlight
of your inner beauty.

So please tell me why
do you want to deny
two people, one love
the harmony and the ecstasy
we create so well,
we sing so well,
we bring out so well
in one another?

Don't try to disguise
your emotions from me
because you forget
I know you,
I feel you,
I breathe you
and it is our destiny
to be together.

Give me the desire
to keep dreaming
through the sunshine
that emerges from
the magic and the voodoo
in your dazzling smile,
the center of my universe.

Don't let the promise
of this love we made,
of this love we bare,
of this love we share
fade...
into oblivion...
you give me life,
you give me hope,
you give me purpose.

Sparkle

Azaleas bloom
beneath the sunrise
that welcomes the arrival
and the promise of a new day
when divine intervention flows
from the Tree of Life
into the ties that bind us
in the joy of friendship.

I discover inspiration
in the comfort of your smile:
an amalgamation
of brilliance, diligence, and patience
that mirrors your genuine spirit
like the pride that blazes
from your bronze skin;
skin that simply expresses
the imperial elegance
of its African heritage
and the strength of a queen
chasing her dreams
in the pursuit of excellence.

To know you
is an honor and a blessing
for you are my sister,
you are my friend.
And I wish you
nothing but the best
in everything you do,
because the Creator's love
is shining upon you.

Miracle

Luminous, laughing eyes
scintillating, smiling face
exuding exuberance,
opening the gateway
into innocence
revealing restless spirits
swirling and swirling,
swirling and swirling
with promise and precocity,
your life, my child
bursting with infinite possibilities;
you are the pride and the reflection
of your parent's love
and the architect of your dreams
to dream big dreams
that exceed the boundaries
of your aspirations
because tomorrow, my child,
belongs to you.

Aftermath

Natural thoughts flow
like rivers and streams
giving life to goals and dreams
when the word is SPOKEN and SLAMMED
into your consciousness
exploding like NAPALM in your face,
awakening sleeping giants in this race,
in this race against time
as brothas and sistas exchange
natural heads and processed minds
for processed heads and natural minds
when followers become leaders
no longer standing
on subway platforms
with their cell phones and laptop Pentiums
waiting for Kings and Tubmans
to rise from the grave,
to take them aboard
the New Underground Railroad
and to lead them
into the next millennium
as their eyes begin to distinguish
the forest from the trees
realizing the tremendous power
residing in the palms of their hands
to transform straw into bricks
and to create glass from sand
when statistics, stereotypes and surroundings
say they can't rise like Maya Angelou
above all challenges and adversities
because they are the Alphas
and the Omegas of their own destiny,

exercising their economic,
financial, and political clout
for the power, the prosperity,
and the preservation of the people
bringing an end to the molestation
and the exploitation of their communities
by the Bushes and the Hilfigers
for their personal profits and agendas
no longer divided
do they fall like
dominoes
and tearing down
each other's reputations
by using degrading words
to erode self esteem like
" BITCH " or " NIGGER, "
united they stand
as one voice, one race
for the empowerment
of a NEW BLACK NATION!

Anointed

I slowly inhale the Breath of Life,
taking my first step along this walk,
marching to the sound of a silent drummer
who speaks to my soul,
giving into sweet surrender
to the rhythm of love,
a supreme love that cannot be
articulated into words,
expressed by deeds,
or translated into thoughts
where tears of joy emerge from my eyes,
washing away the guilt, the anger, and the pain,
releasing the unshackable shackles
from bittersweet memories of days gone by.

I slowly exhale the Breath of Life,
taking my next step along this walk
of GUIDANCE:
God/U and I/DANCE
because this is no easy waltz
and I know the battle
is not mine alone;
as I fall upon bended knees in repentance,
I no longer need to
neither hide in nor chase shadows,
now I rise to my feet
so I stand tall against anything
because the Lord is the light of my life
and the foundation of my existence.

maybe we can …

Today

Creative waters descend
upon the shores of my third eye
as my body and soul
are rocked steady
by the jubilant sounds of
Stevie Wonder's voice
singing "All I Do"
when I envision
iridescent irises
of a light brown hue
tattooed into
my memory
generating tranquil thoughts
that breathe life into
intellectual stimulation
in this time, in this place
where you are
admired and desired
for many moons
to come.

Mystique

Could I be the sunlight
that shines on your face
my dear, sweet sista,
surrounding your cheeks
with a golden glow?
As you stare outside the window
with those brown eyes
bursting with brilliance,
engaged in deep meditation
within your silent sanctuary,
there are some places
a brotha is forbidden to enter
and there are some things
a brotha does not know.

If I could have one wish,
I wish I could enter
the one place I find
most attractive about you
lying in the center
of your imagination
where your ideas and aspirations
are molded,
are sculpted,
and are transformed into
your dreams and reflections
that encompass the essence

of a true
STRONG,
INTELLIGENT,
SELF SUFFICIENT,
TENACIOUS,
AFRICAN GODDESS
that defines you best
from the way
you style your hair
to the clothes you wear,
right down to the pride
and the positive attitude you project
because you are a gift
from the Creator
to be worshipped and adored
for your love is truly precious.

If I could have one chance,
I would love to have the chance
to hold your soft hand
and to let your thoughts flow
from your receptive fingertips into mine,
sending pulsating rhythms
dancing and prancing
throughout my body
with their magical melody,
opening my soul
to respect your emotions,
to appreciate your compassion,
to understand your heartaches
when we look into
each other's eyes
and cherish

the beauty of
SILENCE:
listening to the sounds
of unspoken words
and unsung songs
while inhaling
every breath we take.

Could I be the sunlight
that shines on your face,
my dear, sweet sista,
surrounding your cheeks
with a golden glow?
As you stare outside the window
with those brown eyes
that burst with brilliance,
engaged in deep meditation
within your silent sanctuary,
there are some places
a brotha wants to enter
and there are some things
a brotha needs to know.

So please...
don't...
keep me...
waiting...

Sentimental

Nunca antes
ni en mis sueños más salvajes
habría podido imaginarme
come se siente
el amor bueno
hasta que puse mis brazos
alrededor de tu cintura.

Agarro tu cuerpo al lado del mio
y tu reclinas tu cabeza sobre mi pecho,
escuchando el latido de mi corazón,
sentándonos juntos en la playa arenosa,
observando la salida del sol
sobre el Océano Pacifico.

Soñando despiertos sobre California
un millón de memorias,
trazando y proyectando
mil pensamientos:
dos almas perdidas en el mar
en donde la rima
no tiene ninguna razón
cada día, cada semana,
cada mes, cada temporada
donde encuentro
la ilumanción,
el rejuvenecimiento,
y la salvación
en la fuerza
de tu toque tierno.

Never before in my wildest dreams
could I ever imagined
what good love feels like
until I put my arms
around your waist.

I hold your body next to mine
as you rest your head on my chest,
listening to the sound of my heartbeat,
sitting together on the sandy beach,
watching the sun rise over
the Pacific Ocean.

California daydreaming
one million memories,
plotting and scheming
one thousand thoughts:
two souls lost at sea
where rhyme has no reason
every day, every week,
every month, every season
where I find
illumination,
rejuvenation,
and salvation
in the strength
of your tender touch.

Aurora

Yo te quiero
porque tú eres la luz del sol
de mi vida.

I want you
because you are the sunlight
of my life.

Sexy

You don't need
to take your clothes off
to arouse my desires
because I adore the way
the prominent hue
of your mahogany skin
is accentuated by the flavor
of the tangerine sundress
you wear so well,
and reflects your self-esteem
like incandescent embers
drifting from burning flames
in an ambitious smile
with fearless eyes to match!
You see, that right there
is what turns me on:
your confidence,
yeah, your confidence;
the way you stand alone
like the brightest star
in the sky dancing
amongst the comets
and the constellations
along the stairway to Heaven!
And how you hold yourself
in the highest standards
as a woman, first and foremost,
proud and strong,
recognizing the natural power
of your femininity:
to be the very best
you can be

without
surrendering your soul
or compromising your integrity
to the promiscuous ways
of silver tongued
devils disguised
as men who can
neither control nor conquer
your dreams,
your emotions,
your thoughts,
or your love.

Insomnia

Sleepless
nights without you
find me masturbating
and thinking about you from dusk
'til dawn.

Slide

Running my finger
inside your tulip makes us
feel so wonderful.

Electricity

Contagious sparks surge
through naked bodies bound by
sixty-nine degrees.

27 April 2001

My Queen,

Surprise! I know you weren't expecting this gift but I wanted to give you a little "sumthin' sumthin'" to jump-start your mood for our romantic rendezvous this weekend. And besides, I do know how much you enjoy the amorous sight and the fresh scent of red roses, right? Don't try to hide your smile because I can see the look on your face as you're reading the words from this letter! Ha! ☺

I'm looking forward to tonight because it's been a while, a LONG while, since we've had time for ourselves! I want to celebrate the passion and the promise of the love we share because this will be an evening neither you nor I will forget for the rest of our lives! I know with certainty that I'll constantly replay the moments in my mind for weeks because the feeling is good, so damn good! You don't need to worry about anything but just enjoy yourself and let me cherish the beauty and the ecstasy of you!

Love Always & Forever,

Your King

The Pleasure is Mine

I

I want you
to take your clothes off,
to let your hair down,
and to lie on top of
the black towel I have spread
across our bed
because I can hear
the exhaustion in your voice
that tells me you've had a long day
and all a sista wants to do
is just unwind
because I know
it isn't easy being you,
a strong, positive Black woman
who works hard from
Manic Mondays through Frantic Fridays
where she's overworked and underpaid
and although Corporate America
does not appreciate your efforts,
I do appreciate and respect you
for your desire, determination,
and diligence to succeed,
qualities that give me
the inspiration and the motivation
to be the very best I can be
and make me DAMN proud
to be your man
and with your permission, darling,
I would like to serenade
your sexy body

with a sensuous massage
you will never forget
because tonight,
you are in my hands!

II

Close your eyes,
take a deep breath,
and just relax, my love,
as you inhale the aromatic vapors
of the frankincense
burning and permeating
into the bedroom
while my fingers "do the walking"
on your rich, mahogany skin
because I can feel the tension
beginning to disappear
from your body
like a puddle of water
evaporating in the sunlight
as I caress your gentle shoulders
and rub baby oil into your thighs!
The coo in your voice
is music to my ears
and has me wishing I could
read the pleasant thoughts
inside your mind!
Good vibrations are pulsating
in my body as I stroke
my long fingers
between the cracks
of your tiny toes
and I feel neither shame

nor embarrassment
about my erection
BUILDING AND THROBBING
downstairs
as you drift
into never-never land!

III

Please forgive me, my queen,
when I fantasize
as I touch
your relaxed, soft hair
while you're sleeping,
reminiscing
about the first day we met
and the good times we've shared
but nothing brings me greater joy
when we make
finger snapping, ear popping,
glass shattering, earthshaking love!
The way our body temperatures
rise and reach their boiling point
from the friction of each other's flesh
as your breasts press against my chest
and my hips grind into yours
until we explode like fireworks!
You are love, my angel,
from its flawless beauty
to its simple tranquility
and to know you
and to be a part of your world
is indeed my pleasure!

Good Morning

Sunlight sneaks
through the venetian blinds
and tiptoes across
the baby blue bed sheets
intertwined
between the loving limbs
of two brown bodies
interlocked
like a human jigsaw puzzle
lying naked in
suspended animation
basking in the afterglow
of last night's interlude
when two hearts surrendered
to carnal desires
and made sweet music
together:
"rockin' and rollin',"
"itchin' and scratchin',"
"flippin' and smackin',"
"bumpin' and grindin',"
in a cosmic,
climactic,
orgasmic
collision
when Heaven and Earth
met for the first time.

to all good things ...

Masquerade

Smoke and mirrors create an illusion
weaving webs of total deception
while I disguise the inner turmoil
within my blood which boils
with anger that threatens my salvation,
drawing me closer towards annihilation,
trying to maintain my mental sanity,
drowning in this cesspool called society,
designed to undermine my prosperity
through a facade of blatant dishonesty
while wolves in sheep's clothing
flash their phony smiles
behind their hidden agendas to beguile
decent human beings like you and I
through false promises and lies
to attempt to benefit their needs
bleeding us dry like venomous weeds:
fair weather friends, relatives, former lovers,
acquaintances, politicians, and employers
participating in this deceitful masquerade
as I grow tired of this game of charades.

Clenched Fists

To close my hands in
anger is to throw away
the key to freedom.

Freedom

Dreadlocks
dancing/dangling/dissecting
distinguished airs
of aristocratic societies
as the walls
of capitalistic nations
come crumbling down
to the sounds
of collective voices
screaming for
EMANCIPATION
igniting the movement
of millions across
the African Diaspora:
from the coasts
of North and South America
to the shores of the Caribbean,
across the Motherland
and the European continent,
to the outback of Australia!
A mass Exodus
from mental slavery seeking
REDEMPTION
in the eternal flames
OF BLACK PRIDE
that cannot be
EXTINGUISHED
finding
SALVATION
in the knowledge

of one's self,
of one's past,
of one's value
with open eyes
that decipher the truth
from spoon fed lies
because
WINDS OF CHANGE ARE BLOWIN',
YEAH MON,
WINDS OF CHANGE ARE BLOWIN'!

Timeless

The delightful harmony
of a songbird's symphony
touches my heart in many ways
like the caress of a midsummer's breeze
grazing against my skin
when I close my eyes
and listen to the language
of her lyrics laced with love and languish,
to the prose of her poetry proliferated
with passion and pain
as I shed invisible tears
in reverence for her magnificence
and my soul absorbs
the bittersweet echo
of her voice...
       her voice...
            her voice...
so amazing,
so haunting,
so enchanting,
so outstanding
by blending the best
of raw R&B rhythms
with a cool slice
of sophisticated jazz on the side
celebrating the legacy
of her divine talent that lives on...
and on...
      and on...
         and on...
thank you, Old Friend!

Destiny

I travel alone
down this path
that will lead me
to a destination
unknown,
to a place I call
home
somewhere
at the crossroads
between reality and fantasy
where TIME does not MATTER,
where RACE does not MATTER,
where RELIGION does not MATTER,
where POLITICS does not MATTER,
where ECONOMICS does not MATTER
as FREEDOM RINGS,
as FREEDOM SINGS
through the divine power
that manifests inside of me
and calls upon me
to welcome with open arms
the promise of humanity:
to strive towards peace and harmony
embracing the foundation
of the Creator's love:
the universe and I
become one.

A Moment of Silence

In a moment of silence,
we open our hearts
to feel the rhythm of love
beating/dancing/pulsating
from the rising sun
that adorns the tranquil, blue sky
to the aesthetic colors
tattooed in the tender wings
of a gentle butterfly
as the sounds of angelic souls
sing songs of freedom,
breathing life into better days
where inspiration creates promise;
promise builds strength;
strength rejuvenates faith;
and faith brings hope
that cascades in the carefree,
autumn breeze.

Remember Me

Remember me as the breath of fresh air
you inhale each and every day!

Remember me as the sun's warmth
captured in its golden rays!

Remember me as the shooting star
dancing across the midnight sky!

Remember me as everlasting joy
for the tears in your eyes!

Remember me as a cup of tea
on those days you're feeling blue!

Remember me as your friend
because I'll always remember you!

Dear Bill,

Our time on this planet is coming to an end. Pretty soon you'll be taking that step into another world where you hope to find everlasting joy. I can't say where you're going because I've never been there myself. You've got a 50-50 chance of winding up in one place or another. Although you were neither an angel nor a hell raiser, you've done some things in the past you will have to answer for on Judgment Day. Anyway, you can't dwell on that now. But if you ask me, I think you are going to be in Good hands, my brotha!

Looking back on your "wonder years," I would say you were happy and satisfied with your life. You were an ambitious person who dared to dream big dreams and to challenge yourself by fighting like hell to achieve your goals. You were an optimistic individual who always searched for the good in every person you met, everything you did, and every situation you encountered. You were a leader who strove to be the very best he could be because you recognized the divine nature of life and its infinite possibilities. You had two loving parents, a good brother, a supportive family, and a wonderful group of friends that were always in your corner. And let's not forget, you've met and dated some beautiful and fine ladies (although a few weren't wrapped too tight) and had plenty of unforgettable, romantic nights, which pardon the cliché, "Rocked your world! Hey!"

The achievement in your life that made you most proud was fulfilling your goal of being a writer. You loved to write because it brought you contentment and peace of mind during the good and bad times. You lived to write because it brought out the very best in your artistic creativity. It enabled you to touch places that no one, outside of us, could understand.

You made your mark in this world by touching the lives of your readers. Chances are you won't be remembered in the annals of history like Langston Hughes, Zora Neale Hurston, Walter Mosley, Nikki Giovanni, Alice Walker, Terry McMillan, Eric Jerome Dickey,

Sonia Sanchez, or James Baldwin, but you have so much to be proud of, my brotha. You were a phenomenal poet who wrote some poems that were published in newspapers, magazines, and anthologies. You were not an avaricious person who used his writing to attain monetary gain or sexual pleasures because that was not in your nature. I remember that sentimental feeling you would get in your heart when someone wrote you a letter or sent you an e-mail telling you how he or she was inspired to start writing after they read one of your books. How many times did you want to shed a tear when you saw someone crying after they heard you recite a poem? They knew that someone understood their pain. And don't try to deny the way you could not hold back your enthusiasm when someone gave you a compliment along with a friendly smile. When they said, "I really enjoy your poetry because it is so beautiful, inspiring and honest." Or maybe, "Bill, you are a talented writer," and added, "I loved reading your book." And, of course, the words that touched you most: "Thank you for making me feel special, Bill!"

I'll never forget the famous quote you would always use if anyone ever asked you why you loved to write. You would say, "Every word I write is an extension of my breath, my heart, and my soul that I want the world to share and to remember long after my life has come to an end!"

Believe me, my brotha, your words will be shared and remembered for generations to come. They will be!

Love,

Bill Holmes

poetic dedications/inspirations

desperate times, desperate situations...
- Unbelievable/verdict of the Amadou Diallo trial
- C2D/Lamont Steptoe
- The Cooking Pot/verdict of the James Byrd trial

looking on the bright side...
- Striving/Gail Devers
- Hope/Janet Jackson
- Little Black Boys/Osay Karume and the Twin Poets
- Caribbean Blues/Sandra Walls
- Beauty/Tantra, Sandra Turner Barnes, and D. Ryva Parker

let's keep it together...
- Mama's Smile/Sandra L Baytops
- Dad/William L Holmes Sr. and Larry Baytops
- Heartbeat/Mazie Jones
- Sparkle/Crystal Alston
- Miracle/Christopher Michael and Regina Nichelle
- Aftermath/Lamont "NAPALM" Dixon
- Anointed/Stephanie Lee